DOWN BUT NOT OUT

By W L Croker

INTRODUCTION

I'm not an award-winning author, and I haven't sold millions of copies; this is my first book. I'm just an ordinary girl, mum, wife, daughter, sister, niece, auntie and friend, who like many people, has experienced quite a few challenges in life in a short space of time. Death of loved ones, illness, major surgery, instant hair loss through medication, relationship challenges and so on.

I've had to dig deep and find an inner strength to overcome fear, stress, anxiety and depression. I've learnt how to put on my mask (and sometimes wigs!) to face my family, friends and the world.

I chose a saying, 'meditation before medication', and combined with boxing and yoga, I found the light at the end of the tunnel was thankfully 'not' a train coming towards me!

The sayings in this book I've mostly made up myself and some I've learned along the way from the interesting people I've met. My hope is that it will inspire people from all walks of life, at different times in their lives and hopefully raise money for my chosen charity, with all proceeds going to 'Cancer Research'.

Dear 'bad times'
Thank you for the inspiration
For giving me the motivation
To achieve my goals with dedication
And maybe even admiration!
You have given me the determination to
accept your lessons with appreciation!
(I may not have done it without you!)

— — — — — — — —

With loving thanks to all my family, friends, doctors,
nurses , hospital staff, teachers and ANGELS for all
your kindness and support, too many names to
mention, you know who you are…

Thank you so much

xxx

Dear Cancer

You took her breast

You took her hair

You came without warning

You clearly don't care

Whose lives you take

and those you destroy!

Whether it be, a girl or a boy

Men and women, husbands and wives

All determined to save their lives!

They love to hear the words 'all clear'

They have got rid of you, but not the 'fear!'

After the surgery, the treatment is rough

They're pushed to the limit and have to be tough

Then... bang, now they are in menopause

Now that is a whole new set of rules!

You can't have this

Don't take that

No H.R.T, just get fat!

Whilst they're down

They're kicked in the head

Life goes on

You can't stay in bed

Hot sweats, low mood, now you need glasses

You look around, whilst life passes

Those around you, don't understand

The tsunami's passed, but

Who clears up the land?

So go away Cancer

and don't come back

If you were a job, you'd get the sack!

Researcher, doctor or nurse

All working tirelessly to remove your curse!

We will fight you

and never give in

You may be strong, but you won't win!

Cures are improving

The public are moving

Coming together in all kinds of weather

What's it about?

We're working it out

Is it our food?

Or what we drink?

You have made the world sit up and think

Is it the Wifi or radiation?

Nuclear waste or the power station?

Whatever it is and wherever you are

We're stopping it now

You won't go far.....

by Wendy Croker

xx

My nan used to say that cures are found in nature, it's not a coincidence that dock leaves grow near stinging nettles!

Find people that you can completely 'be yourself' around, they are your REAL FRIENDS

Life is like a book. Be your own author, write the next chapter, make it a good one

The main difference
between winners and
losers is belief!
Whatever you believe, you
will be right!

Let go of perfection, it doesn't exist in nature!

We can't always choose what happens to us but we can choose how we respond to it!

Accept that we all have different skills, don't think less of an elephant if it struggles to climb a tree!

Visits always give pleasure, if not the coming of someone, then the going of them!

We learn as much from the people we don't get on so well with, as the ones that we do!

Even if they teach us how we don't want to be!

When you have a problem in life, try and think what lesson it's teaching you, try to learn from it the first time round, to save you being sent back to learn it again!

Water the flowers and not the weeds!

Greatness is not always
about accomplishment,
but how you deal
with adversity!

Sometimes we are taken to muddy waters, not to drown, but to cleanse!

Don't dwell on negative thoughts, remember there is no future in the past!

Don't be so busy focusing on the problem, that you forget to find a solution!

People who chop bricks with their bare hands don't see the brick, they see beyond the brick.
When faced with a problem, see yourself smiling when you've solved it!

Don't be an approval
seeker, you're here once,
do it your way!

Don't buy a ticket for the 'aggro' bus, let it drive past!

You can love material
things but they will never
love you back!

Worrying about something that hasn't happened yet is like paying interest on a loan you never took out!

Nothing new can be grown, if you stay in your comfort zone!

Education is a worthwhile investment. Unlike material things, it can't be taken away from you!

I was only ever comfortable with giving, until someone told me if you don't like to receive, you're denying some else the pleasure of giving. Now I'm ok with both!

If you can't help someone up the hill in difficult times, then try not to be a rucksack on their back!

Be selfless, not selfish!

Imagine that everyone is
wearing a badge that says
'make me feel important'

Without disappointment,
you cannot
appreciate victory!

When your car skids on the road, you're taught to straighten up and keep focused on where you were going. Don't get thrown off balance.

Do the same in life!

I've never known an argument to start with a compliment!

You can handle anything
that is temporary.
Everything is temporary!

People make mistakes, that is why cars have bumpers and pencils have rubbers!

It's not how beautiful you are that counts. It's how beautiful you think you are!

You don't know how strong you are, until you need to be!

Everyone says be strong
and positive. Good advice,
but you are allowed
a day off!

When you have seen the dark side of life, you get to really appreciate the light!

Never worry that someone
is better than you at
something.
Nothing in life is equal.

Be a leader, but remember that a leader doesn't have to lead from the front!

Imagine you are an oak tree. Your branches may sway in the wind, stay grounded, learn to weather all storms!

10 COMMANDMENTS OF PARENTHOOD

1. Listen to your children, show them love

2. Ignore them when they're naughty (expect in danger) praise them when they're good!

3. Have a few rules and stick to them.

4. Don't shout, talk quietly. That way, they'll need to listen hard to hear you.

5. Teach them good manners, it's nice to be nice!

6. Remember 'old fashioned' play. Bikes, scooters, hide and seek, exercise and social skills.

7. Teach them to ignore rude and hurtful comments, never take them personally, whoever is being mean, is just trying to deflect their own negative feelings.

8. Let food and laughter be your first medicine.

9. Honesty. The worst truth is better than a lie.

10. Mindfulness. Live in the moment, be happy, enjoy life!

RULES AND TOOLS FOR LIFE
(may seem obvious…)

1. Focus on the positive and what you want, not what you don't want!

2. Don't take unnecessary risks!

3. Believe in yourself.

4. Be happy and healthy.

5. Believe compliments, ignore negativity.

6. Find out what you're good at and what you love doing and do it as much as you can!

7. Don't deal with liars or cheats.

8. Let go of what you can't control.

9. Speak your mind, you can't be wrong and strong!

10. Be kind and help others less fortunate.

NAMASTE

(The light in you honours
the light in me!)

Printed in Great Britain
by Amazon